Puzzling Frame Games

BY TERRY STICKELS

Scholastic Inc.

New York   Toronto   London   Auckland   Sydney
Mexico City   New Delhi   Hong Kong   Buenos Aires

ISBN 0-439-38878-3

12 11 10 9 8 7 6 5 4 3 2 1   2 3 4 5 6 7/0

Printed in the U.S.A.   40
First printing, November 2002

CONTENTS

INTroductioN

Frame Games are puzzles that are just as much fun to create as they are to solve. By placing letters, numbers, and pictures in a box, well-known phrases, names, places, and song titles are expressed. You can have hours of fun both solving frame games and creating your own. Here's an example:

The answer is "**circles under the eyes**." The letters and words in each frame game may involve different shapes, like circles, triangles, or squares, or different positions, like high, low, or slanting. Here's another one:

**PINEAPPLE
CAKE**

The answer is "**Pineapple upside-down cake**."

Don't worry if it takes you some time to get the feel of how to solve these puzzles. Some frame games are more difficult than others. But you'll be amazed at how quickly you'll start to discover the answers.

After a while, try creating your own puzzles. Your friends and family will have just as much fun solving your frame games as you will have solving mine.

Have fun, and I wish you happy frame game solving!—T.S.

Easy

SAVED

self-stm

better, better,
better, better
or
WORSE

needle

N◉SE

YR act

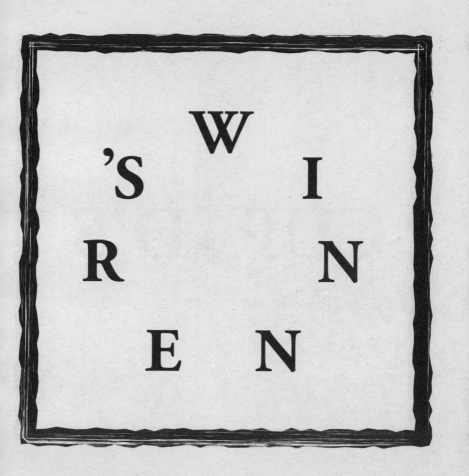

CUPID'S

STRU🌙K

young@heart

_____ walk

DRER

brithey

MEdium

MAKING
ENDEND

STAY

Sir Lance, Lance, Lance, Lance, Lance, Lance...

NOWHERE

meals **BRUSH** meals

GOLDEN

GOLDEN

GOLDEN

GOLDEN

GOLDEN

RICHES

HELPING HELPING

CAKES

The . home

PANTS

M+M+M+M
family

cover
cover **HEAD** cover
cover

apl youryour ¢¢¢

a cut

He's   the rest.

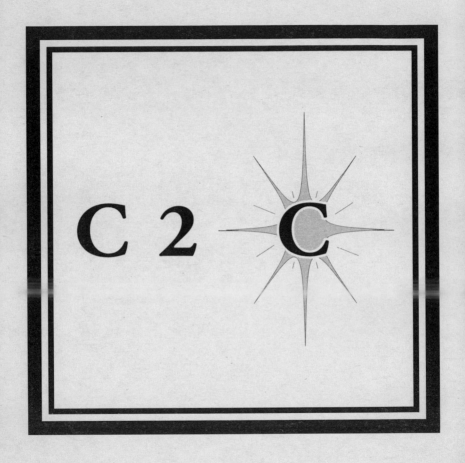

EEEEEE THE ROAD

SHREDS

SHREDS

DRESSING

HIS
DEAD
TRACKS

a, b, c, d, e, f, g, h

TRAFFIC

the last
word ÷ 2

```
        W
P  sunglasses  R
        A
```

it it it
it it
it BELL it
it it
it it it

E 10 ALIVE

B10 @ the YR

flight

so

GOING 4

PARKING

PARKING

ChALLenGinG

VESTSEV

LIES
LIES   FEAR

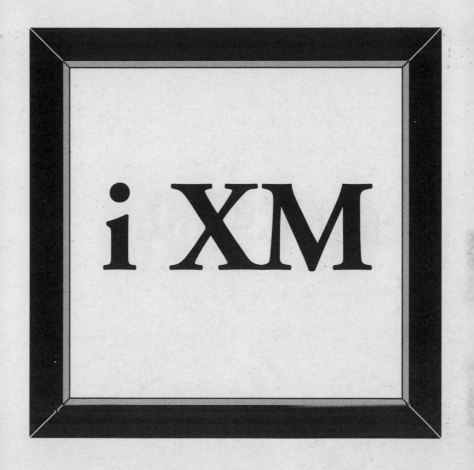

put 12" other

side —

looking

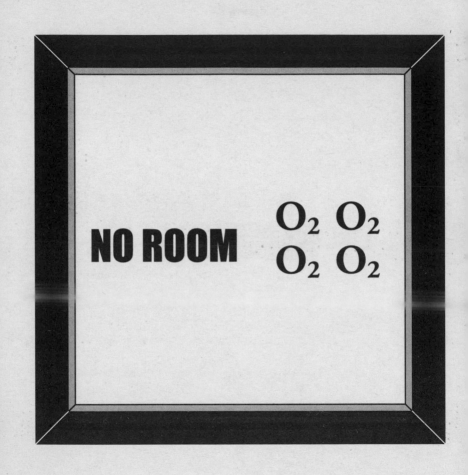

YROTCIVYROTCIV

Answers

Answers to Easy Frame Games

p. 8 — Saved by the bell

p. 9 — Paint by numbers

p. 10 — Thickheaded

p. 11 — High self–esteem

p. 12 — For better or worse

p. 13 — Surf the web

p. 14 — Chicago White Sox

p. 15 — Razor thin

p. 16 — Eye of the needle

p. 17 — Button nose

p. 18 — Tooth decay

p. 19 — Weak link

p. 20 — Road work ahead

p. 21 — High-wire act

p. 22 — Stretch limo

p. 23 — Winner's circle

p. 24 — Cupid's arrow

p. 25 — Moonstruck

p. 26 — Face the music

p. 27 — Young at heart

p. 28 — Space walk

p. 29 — Hair dryer

p. 30 — Britney Spears

Answers to Medium Frame Games

p. **32** – Candy striper

p. **33** – Big Dipper

p. **34** – Two peas in a pod

p. **35** – Making ends meet

p. **36** – Tilt-a-Whirl

p. **37** – Stay on track

p. **38** – Cliff-hanger

p. **39** – Sir Lancelot

p. **40** – Jaywalking

p. **41** – The middle of nowhere

p. **42** – Brush between meals

p. **43** – It just crossed my mind

p. **44** – Five golden rings

p. **45** – From rags to riches

p. **46** – Second helping

p. **47** – Crab cakes

p. **48** – Clean sweep

p. **49** – Hammer the point home

p. **50** – Me and my shadow

p. **51** – Sweatpants

p. **52** – Addams family

p. **53** – Head for cover

p. **54** – Seeing Eye™ dog

Answers to Hard Frame Games

Answers to Challenging Frame Games

p. 80 — Closing in on the solution

p. 81 — Reversible vest

p. 82 — Split-level homes

p. 83 — Custer's last stand

p. 84 — Paralyze with fear

p. 85 — Archangels

p. 86 — Solid citizen

p. 87 — Eye exam

p. 88 — Put one foot in front of the other

p. 89 — From the outside looking in

p. 90 — No room left for error

p. 91 — Back-to-back victories